MASTERING ART

COLLAGE

Anthony Hodge

STARGAZER BOOKS

CONTENTS

© Aladdin Books Ltd 2005

New edition published in the United States in 2005 by:
Stargazer Books
c/o The Creative Company
123 South Broad Street
P.O. Box 227
Mankato, Minnesota 56002

Design: Phil Kay
Editors: Nicola Cameron, Jen Green
Drawings: Anthony Hodge
Illustrations: Ron Hayward Associates

Printed in UAE
All rights reserved

Library of Congress Cataloging-in-Publication Data

Hodge, Anthony
    Collage / Anthony Hodge. -- New ed.
        p. cm. -- (Mastering art)
    Includes index.
    ISBN 1-932799-03-6
    1. Collage--Technique--Juvenile literature. I. Title.

N7433.7.H63 2004
702'.81'2--dc22   2004040165

Introduction

Collage, a French word meaning pasting or gluing, is a very flexible art form. It can take you beyond the limitations of paints and brushes, and introduce you to a new world of creative picture making.

Everyone can do it

Collage can be quick and easy. It makes use of ready-made materials like photographs and paper, and is good for anyone who enjoys making images. Collage can go hand in hand with drawing and painting, or can be a separate activity in its own right.

New from old

Collage is cheap; it uses things people often think of as garbage. The materials you need are all around you and can cost next to nothing. Collage is about combining familiar things in new and original ways.

About this book

This book begins with a guide to tools, techniques, and materials. With the aid of projects, it guides you through simple image-making, to a series of more advanced techniques.

▶ "Scraps of styrofoam and candy box paper suggest this snow scene. I used string for the broomstick and plants, corrugated cardboard for the house, and bubble wrap packing for the falling snow."

Tearing and Cutting

The next pages introduce some basic tools and techniques for paper collage. To get paper to the shape you require, you will need to tear or cut it. There are many ways of accomplishing this first step of collage-making.

Tearing

It is very simple to pick up a piece of paper and tear a shape out of it. A torn edge can look very pleasing, both on its own or when placed next to a cut edge. Torn paper can often look surprisingly effective, once you've placed it in position.

Cutting

The main tools for cutting are scissors and craft knives. Used skillfully, they can both produce a variety of curved and straight lines.

A craft knife can cut shapes in paper as easily as a pencil can draw them. But a craft knife is sharp, so always cut away from your body. Make sure the safety cover is replaced after use.

A cutting surface

If you're using a craft knife, you will need something to cut on. Cardboard will do, but it must be thick. Rubber cutting mats are quite expensive, but will never wear out.

◄ The blue figure is torn from paper that is colored on both sides. The torn edges will be a lighter shade and have a different texture.

The pink figure is torn from paper that is colored on one side only. If you tear a piece in half, one of the strips will have a colored edge, and the other will have a white edge. This can look effective against a background of a different color.

▲ A hole punch can be used to create interesting effects. Here, holes in blue paper create the effect of falling snow.

▼ Special scissors called pinking shears create a regular V-shaped edge that can look like grass.

▲ A craft knife produces clean lines. It is also good for cutting holes in the middle of paper, like the castle windows above.

▶ Folding or curling can make flat paper three-dimensional. The steps above were folded and the bird's plume was curled around a pencil. A torn straight edge can be created by tearing paper against a ruler. Scissors or a craft knife can be used to fringe paper.

Special Effects with Paper

Paper is a very flexible material that can be used in many different ways. Some of the special effects you can achieve are described here; you may be able to think of some new ones.

Changing texture

Paper usually has an even, uniform surface. But this texture, or feel, can be changed. Thin paper, such as tissue paper, can be scrunched up and then flattened out again. Paper can also be pressed onto rough or textured surfaces and rubbed with a hard object like the back of a spoon to give it a different feel.

With tinfoil you can create the impression of an object by wrapping foil around it and then lifting it off. The spoon below is an example.

▼ "The collage below uses a number of techniques to produce a picture of the objects found on a kitchen table. I have scrunched up purple tissue paper to imitate the skin of the prunes. To simulate the pitted surface of strawberries, I pressed red paper over a sieve and rubbed it with a spoon."

Fixing Paper Down

Drawing and painting
Try drawing or painting on parts of the paper to create a range of different effects. Colored pencils, crayons, chalks, felt-tip markers, and paints can all be used for this.

Gluing paper down
Once your paper is torn or cut and painted, you will need to attach it to the background of your collage. Gluing is the basic method. Most glues dry to a clear surface. Any glue left showing can be rubbed off.

▲ "Above is a fruit bowl collage made with a combination of cut and torn shapes, painted and attached in various ways. I used thumbtacks and staples in the picture to resemble pits and stalks of fruit."

Tape, thumbtacks, and staples
Tape can be used to fix paper down. Use double-sided tape on the back if you don't want it to show. You can use thumbtacks and staples to attach heavier papers to cardboard, styrofoam, or cork.

The World of Paper

Paper is the most important resource for a collage artist. From tissue paper to newsprint, from postcards to writing paper, it's important to get to know the range of papers that are available.

A library of paper

For this project you will need to collect lots of different types of paper.

The aim is to discover what can be done with paper by putting together your own collage of petal shapes using different papers. Use as many textures as you can find.

Practicing composition

If you pick a bunch of flowers, you will probably want to arrange them in a vase. In the same way, your paper flowers need to be arranged in a pleasing way. This is called composition. An advantage of collage is the ability to practice composition before deciding on and fixing down a final version.

▶ "I have overlapped some flowers on the right. Using similar shapes will highlight the different qualities and textures of the paper."

All about paper

The word "paper" comes from the name of the papyrus plant that grew wild along the Nile River, in Egypt, about 4,000 years ago. Ancient Egyptians would pound the leaves flat and use them to write on.

Today, almost all of the paper you use is made of wood fibers. Wood fibers consist of tiny cellulose strands attached together with a natural adhesive material called lignin. By separating and reorganizing these fibers, paper is made. Shown here are
(1) corrugated paper, (2) notepaper, (3) tracing paper, (4) recycled paper, and (5) gift wrap.

9

Step by Step

Gathering your ingredients
Collage can involve a wide range of materials. This project is about working with more varied ingredients, and building a picture with them step by step.

Begin by assembling your raw materials. You might collect ready-made images, like postcards and photographs from magazines. You could also include different types of paper.

▼ 1. A mixture of torn and cut edges will add interest to your picture. Your paper shapes can be overlapped. Keep an open mind about where, and at what angle, the pieces might go.

▼ 2. Magazine images add color and texture to your work. Remember that you can make alterations to your pictures before, and even after, fixing them down.

◄ "Here are some of the materials I used for the jungle collage. I added some interesting odds and ends-bits of packaging material and other scraps of junk that would otherwise have been thrown away."

Finding a subject

You may have an idea for your collage before you start, or an idea may come to you as you gather materials. To begin your collage, cut and tear simple shapes for some of the main themes in your collage (1).

Size and scale

Picture postcards and photographs (2) provide images for you to experiment with scale. Objects that are close to us look large, and those that are farther away look smaller. Look at the images of animals on the left. The largest, the lion, belongs in the foreground of the picture. The medium-sized gorilla looks right in the middle, and the tiny bird looks best at the top, where it appears to be in the distance.

Putting it all together

It's time to see how your materials fit together (3). The odds and ends can be added to the picture for a three-dimensional look and a touch of humor. The elements of your collage are like a puzzle, but there is no right or wrong way to put them together. See what looks best to you.

▼ 3. Below is a finished collage. A bottle top has become the sun, and a piece of string has turned into a snake sunning itself on a rock. Strong glue was needed to fix these down securely.

Working with Color

One of the joys of collage is being able to work with large areas of color, without first having to mix paint, or to crayon laboriously. There's no better way to find out how colors work together.

Colors have many jobs to do

Colors express feeling and create mood and atmosphere. Colors can blend together or stand out. Colors can appear to change depending on which other colors they are placed next to. Warm colors, such as yellows and reds, seem to jump out, whereas cool colors, such as blues and purples, are more retiring. By positioning colors correctly, you can create a real sense of depth in your work.

Creating depth with color

This project works best with tissue paper as it allows colors to show through one another.

To build up a land or a seascape, begin by laying down broad areas of color. Use warm colors in the foreground, and cooler colors in the background. Overlapping colors creates subtle shades, like the turquoise at the water's edge in the collage shown, which suggests shallower water.

▶ "To get the tissue paper to lie flat, I put small spots of glue on either end of the torn strips and smoothed them down. Once the background was finished, I added finer details, such as the sun, the boat, and the swimmers, to focus the eye on the different areas of the picture."

▼ Warm colors advance toward you. They look better in the foreground of your picture. Cool colors recede; they fit best in the background of the picture.

▼ The eye is drawn to contrasting, or complementary colors, such as yellow and purple. Other contrasting pairs are red and green, and blue and orange.

▼ A single layer of transparent yellow or red paper laid over a white background looks pale and muted; a double layer looks darker and brighter. Overlapping different colors creates new ones. Here, red and yellow are overlapped to make orange.

13

Exploring Tone

What is tone? Tone suggests how light or dark something is. Tone gives shape to objects by showing where light falls on them. This project is about practicing seeing tone by making a collage from newspaper.

Tone and lighting

Arrange some objects into a still life, such as bottles and a glass on a table. The two factors that affect the tones are the colors of your objects—how light or dark they are—and the effect of light on them. For example, a pale highlight on a black pitcher could look lighter than a shadow on a white plate.

Matching tone

Study the effect of light on your arrangement and identify areas of tone in it. Look closely at the bottles and the glass on the table. Match what you see with the black, gray, and white tones of your newspaper. Cut or tear shapes from paper of the right tone, and build up your picture.

▶ "From the large black letters of the headlines, to widely spaced lettering and small print, a newspaper contains all the tones you need for your still life. To make the job simpler, I put the background in first, and the paler shapes over it."

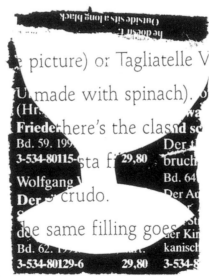

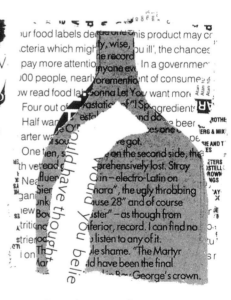

▲ A light shining from the side creates areas of pale tone and shadow on an object. Sometimes, these are very distinct.

▲ If you place light and dark tones next to one another, it produces a dramatic effect. The eye is drawn to these areas.

▲ Cut shapes often convey abrupt changes in tone. A torn line can suggest one area of tone blurring into another.

▲ All colors have tones. If you look at the squares here, you may be able to identify particular colors, and the differences between their tones. Compare them to the tones on the newspaper. The more you look, the more tones you will see in the newspaper.

Marbling and Rubbing

Marbling paper is fun, and can produce amazing results for you to use in collage. You will need oil paint, linseed oil, turpentine, a bowl, some jelly jars, and a cover for your working surface.

Rubbings

Rubbings are impressions of textures. Look for objects with interesting textures. Place a sheet of thin paper over one, and rub the paper with colored crayon, pencil, or chalk.

Marbling

Follow the steps below and you can make some interesting patterns.

▶ Use your rubbings and marbled papers to make a collage, perhaps a landscape, like the one on the right.

▲ In a jelly jar, mix one teaspoonful of linseed oil with two of turpentine. Add six inches of paint from a tube, and stir the mixture with a stick.

▲ Make up several jelly jars with different colors. Fill a bowl with water. Pour in a jar of paint. The mixture will float on the water. Stir it again.

▲ Take a piece of plain paper and lay it on the surface of the water. Lift it off again almost immediately, and drain off the excess water. Lie it flat to dry.

▲ Your paper will now be marbled. You can immerse it again in another color, or add a new color to the water and try again with a fresh sheet of paper.

Making a good impression

Below are some examples of different textures made by rubbing. Try making rubbings of coins and the grain of wood.

Many kitchen utensils also have interesting textures—try a cheese grater, a sieve, or a straw place mat.

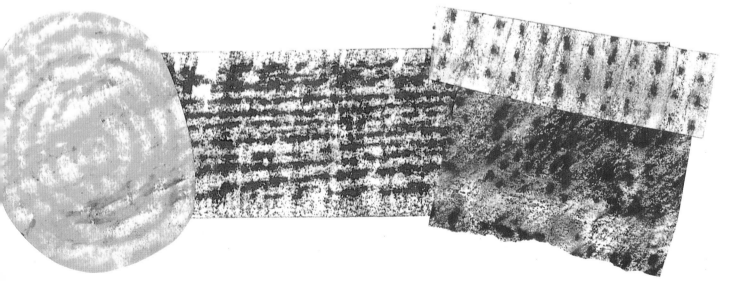

Working with Photos

"From this day on, painting is dead." Many people believed this when photography was invented. Artists today haven't given up painting, but a great many use photographs in picture-making.

Picture puzzles

Cutting up and reassembling pictures will produce new images that can be intriguing and funny. You will need a collection of images cut from photographs or magazines. Cut the images into squares, strips, or a shape like a fan. A fan shape can emphasize curves, such as a goose's neck.

Two into one *will* go

The project at the bottom of the opposite page works best with two images that complement each other. Cut both pictures into strips, combine the two images, and the shapes will interact with one another.

▲ The image above is composed of squares. To cut squares more accurately, mark out the lines on the back of your image first.

The illustration shows just one of the many ways in which the squares can be reassembled. Try rotating each square by 90° and see what happens. Try again, rotating all the squares by 180° and sticking them down.

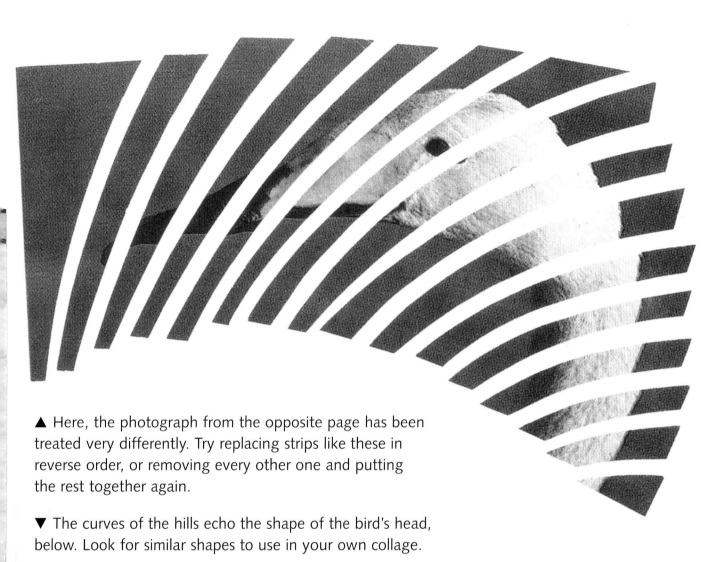

▲ Here, the photograph from the opposite page has been treated very differently. Try replacing strips like these in reverse order, or removing every other one and putting the rest together again.

▼ The curves of the hills echo the shape of the bird's head, below. Look for similar shapes to use in your own collage.

Photomontage

A collage made up of a number of photographs is called a photomontage. Photomontages can often look more like pictures of dreams than of everyday life. Shapes can be repeated, and familiar images can be bizarrely transformed. This project explores the patterns you can make with repeated shapes. You will need a craft knife and photographs or magazines.

Repeating shapes

Look through your photographs and magazines to find an image that appeals to you. Choose a figure or a simple form that is easy to recognize from its outline or silhouette alone. Cut around the outline, pressing down hard on the magazine and cutting through several other pages as you do so. Once you've cut out your outline, you will be left with a series of identical shapes (see the illustration below).

On the left below, the figure on the balcony (1) has been cut out and moved from its original setting (2), leaving the negative shape.

On the right, both figures and backgrounds have been turned over, to produce a series of shapes that mirror those on the left.

Positive and negative

You will also have a number of holes in the backgrounds, or "negative shapes," in addition to the positive ones of the figure itself. The idea is to include both the positive and negative shapes in your collage and see what kind of image you can create.

Magazines are printed on both sides of the paper, so your positive and negative images will have parts of other pictures printed on the back of them. Collect a series

▲ "I have put single leaves together in a group to transform them into whole trees. A cat's face has become a butterfly; its shape echoes the floating features of the face on the opposite side."

of images and backgrounds. The montage above is based on the mirroring technique, and also on the dream-like transformation of one thing into another. Turn some over and see how they mirror the others.

Drawing with Collage

Your collage projects have so far involved the assembly and cutting of materials to produce a variety of compositions. In this project, a drawing or painting is supplemented by collage techniques.

Using collage fragments

Choose a subject for your drawing. This subject could be a street scene or the view from a window. See how you can add to your drawing. Newspaper headlines, newsprint clippings, and magazine ads can all enhance your drawing. Don't take the words on your fragments too literally—they don't necessarily need to correspond with your subject.

Mixing materials

The picture opposite was drawn in pencil, charcoal, brown oil pastel, and pen and ink. Leave spaces in your drawing for your collage fragments. Try different compositions with your newspaper clippings. Once you have finished, glue them in place to complete your picture.

▶ If your subject is a street scene, printed words and pictures can add a touch of realism to store fronts, signs, or billboards. If you find drawing people difficult, why not make them with collage instead?

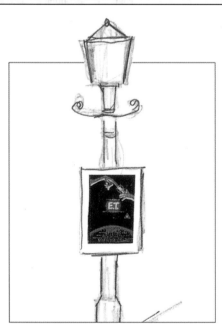

▲ To avoid smudging, spray your drawing with fixative before you add in your chosen fragments.

▲ Alternatively, fix down your collage paper first. You can draw an image around it, without smudging.

▲ If you can't find a word, cut out separate letters and paste them down to spell the word out.

Working with Fabric

You don't have to be able to sew or knit to enjoy the rich world of cloth. Fabrics open up an entirely new range of possibilities, enabling you to achieve effects you can't get any other way.

Many textures

Collect as many different kinds of fabric as you can find. Silk, corduroy, velvet, burlap, muslin, wool, and felt—each material has its own weave, texture, and pattern. Buttons, sequins, and lace can be added. You will need a pair of sharp scissors, strong glue, pins or staples, and thick cardboard or cork to use as a base for your collage.

What do your scraps suggest?

Study your pieces and see what they remind you of. You could try a head like the one here, a landscape, or an abstract pattern. Try your pieces in different positions before sticking or stapling them to your base.

▼ "The scraps of fabric I collected suggested the crazy face and clothes of a clown. I chose white nylon for the face and a background of cotton drill, and began by laying down these basic ingredients.

I chose shiny red cotton for the clown's nose, and small cotton patchwork squares for his jacket. I tried strands of wool for the hair, but finally chose a coarse tweed material instead."

Three-dimensional Collage

Throughout this book, in gluing one piece of paper over another, you have been creating an image that is three-dimensional. This project is about developing this quality fully, and creating an image that really stands out!

A load of old garbage

You will need to make a new collection, this time of junk! Old boxes, tubes, plastic bottles, toys, wood, and leaves can all be used. You will need a base of wood, cork, or styrofoam. Nails, staples, or glue will fix the objects in place. Choose a subject—it could be a science fiction city scene with stairways and towers as shown here.

Using shadows

One of the advantages of 3-D collage is that the shadows cast by objects can become part of the design. When it's all fixed down, a coat of paint will unify your collage, and emphasize the play of light and shadow on it.

▶ Nails, pine cones, bark, and the imprint of a car in tinfoil have all been used on the right. The toys add a bit of extra interest.

Adapting your materials

Some of your ingredients will need to be transformed before they can be used. Open out some boxes, halve tubes, and splay out plastic cups. Fold card to make steps and doors. Hide things inside others.

A Diary in Collage

It's said that every picture tells a story. Have you ever kept a scrapbook of a vacation you went on that reminds you of the trip? This project uses the souvenirs collected on such a journey to make a three-dimensional collage.

Scrapbook journalism

If you have an old scrapbook, this is an opportunity to recycle all your old vacation souvenirs. If not, you will need to go on a special expedition to gather your materials. Try a trip to a gallery or a walk in the park and see what you you can find.

On your expedition

Plan a journey on which you are likely to find the materials you need. Tickets, maps, flyers, and picture postcards are just some of the souvenirs that might be effective in a collage. Take snapshots, or draw sketches. You could decide to stop regularly, every hundred paces, for example, and draw or pick up anything that looks interesting. The things you collect could be paper, balloons, coins, film, and sand.

Composing your materials

When you get home, arrange your materials on a large sheet of cardboard, or on a firm base. Try your objects in different positions. You may decide to make a composition using objects in the order in which they were collected. Or you may choose a more abstract composition. When you find the most pleasing composition, fix down your materials. Many modern artists have presented records of their journeys in this way.

◄ "My collage records a trip to Disneyworld, but as you can see, the work is still in progress. Most of the materials have been positioned, but the objects bottom right have yet to become part of the picture."

Your own collage might include some of the materials below—brochures and picture postcards, maps, tickets, and passes. You could also use "found objects" such as twigs, leaves, flowers, earth, and shells.

Gifts and Presentation

Collage offers a great way to produce many kinds of images, in bulk. These images can make excellent cards and posters.

Repeating yourself
By pressing hard through several layers of paper with a craft knife, or by cutting them with scissors, you can create a series of identical shapes. These shapes can be used to mass-produce cards or posters. On the left are identical posters for a school play, that were made in this way.

Varying composition
Identical shapes don't have to be arranged in the same way every time. On the right, two party invitations are made with identical images but have different compositions. The shapes have been positioned at opposite angles, and even affixed upside down. Glue your paper shapes onto stiff cardboard for better results.

Presentation
Your collages will look even better when well presented. Some will look good with trimmed edges, mounted on cardboard, or framed behind glass. If your collage is made of freely torn shapes, the rough edges may look best untrimmed, mounted with a border of cardboard showing on all sides.

Practical Tips

Storing your materials

Many of the projects in this book have involved collecting materials, so you need to organize some storage space. Sort different kinds of paper into separate piles, and store them neatly.

Preparation

Collage can be untidy and messy, so you will need a lot of space to work in. Cover your working area with old cloths and wear old clothes. Keep paper towels at hand in case of spills. Replace the cap on your tube of glue, and cover your craft knife.

Gluing large areas

If you need to glue large areas of paper, wallpaper paste is ideal. The paste should be mixed with water in a jar.

Warning

The fumes from some kinds of glue are harmful. Be very careful not to breathe them in.

More tearing techniques

You can get a neat tear by lightly scoring a line in your paper first with a craft knife. Tear along the scored line for a slightly ragged edge, or press out the shape instead. Alternatively, draw the line you want with a paintbrush dipped in water, and then tear along it while the paper is still wet.

At a distance

Collages are pictures too, and they need the chance to be seen in their own right. Hang your work on a wall where it can be seen from a distance. Over a period of time, you may notice things you want to change. One of the great advantages of collage is that additions and alterations are nearly always possible.

Index